nolo contendere

Judson Crews

Preface by
Robert Creeley

drawings by
Lori Felton

Edited by J. Whitebird

Acknowledgments

None of the poems in this book
have been published previously.
Back cover illustration by Giam
Buu Truong. Typesetting by
Public Works, Inc.

© 1978 Wings Press
Printed in the U.S.A.

Library of Congress 78-73263

ISBN   0-930324-08-0 (Hardback)
        0-930324-09-9 (Paperback)

WINGS PRESS
P.O. Box 25296
Houston, Texas 77005
713-668-7953

PREFACE

It's presumption indeed to interrupt another man's altogether competent conversation, especially before he's even had chance to begin. But—Judson Crews is a modest man and a most honest one, and he won't tell you himself what I think you have right and reason to know. For one thing, he is a man of absolute principle, by which I mean that he has taken explicit care to consider the world and he has come to some conclusions—not to lie, not to cheat, not to murder, not to kick one's fellows when they're down. You'd be surprised how few people ever get around to thinking about such things, much less to taking a stand.

For years Mr. Crews lived in Ranchos de Taos, New Mexico, with his wife and two daughters, working as a pressman for the local newspaper at one dollar an hour. At the same time he published a number of little magazines, **Suck Egg Mule**, **Poetry Taos**, **The Naked Ear**, among them, and a series of his own books—and usually he put a photo reproduction of a naked lady in each one, as much as to say, if you can't 'understand' these poems, you might test your powers on this person; i.e., I'm sure that God loves us all.

Coming from the east, I had a larger than lifesize sense of Texans. When we were still kids, a friend of my father's just back from Texas brought us a donkey in a taxicab from Boston, after having got it that far by train. So it was clearly a real place, and when I later read of the Alamo and who was there, and how they literally held out till the last man went down, I hoped one day to know the people of that state because it seemed they might well be a little bigger, a bit more ample, more generous, and factually finer than their somewhat bedraggled countrymen. Sadly the events of the past twenty years have cut that dream down to very meager size —and I'm sure we've all met a lot of Texans, like they say. But I'd still like to remember, as a company, Sam Houston, Robert Rauschenberg, Janis Joplin, Judson Crews, and Freebelly Norton, just that he **was** the first Texan I ever met (it was the Second World War) and certainly he was no disappointment.

So what does this have to do with Mr. Crews' poems? A great deal, in fact. You can't make an omelet without breaking eggs. You can't get an egg to break without a chicken to lay it. Mr. Crews is not so simply an autobiographical writer, and I don't know whether or not he's done all the things he talks of in these poems. I'm damn sure someone has—and that their wry, laconic, sensitive perception is fact of very human experience. **Integrity** is a very apt word for Judson Crews' way of being human. He won't do what he doesn't believe in doing, nor will he say something for simple convenience. That's cost him a lot at times, jobs included, but you can no more be a little bit committed to telling the veritable truth than you can be a little bit pregnant. So you might as well go for broke.

One day, when we're all, as Jack Kerouac put it, "safe in Heaven, dead," I'm sure that Judson Crews will be both remembered and honored for the loner wisdom of what he had to tell us and that wild down-home elegance of what one might call his delivery. Like in that knife fight when the one guy says, you never touched me!—and the other says, just try to move your head—maybe it will take time to catch up with this dear man's delights. But if you're reading this, you're surely getting close. Onward!

Robert Creeley

Placitas, New Mexico
June 30, 1978

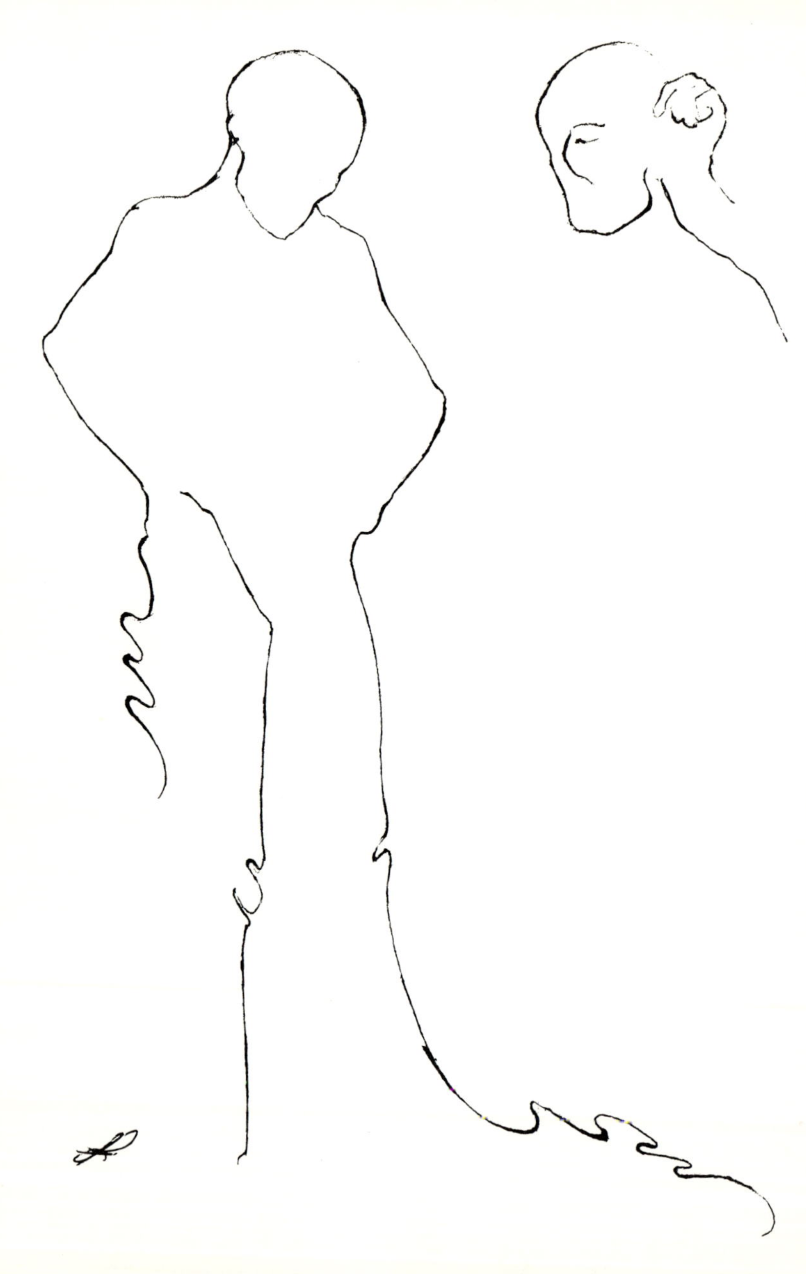

nolo contendere

A poem

Can't quite be
that clean

A light plane
and a dark

A trace of shading
proving affinity

A metaphysics

Of donkey
            entrails
the conundrum

Of his black
            cods
yes, we

Hear him
          braying
at dawn

When the
          pearly light
is grey

Upon his
          grey
pelt, ears

Erect for
          an answer
maybe

Her nakedness in

A field of light
              her whiteness
solarized on a ground of daybreak
the vigour of her strong loins
her arms light as heaven
                          her buttocks
glorious as basilisks

Her nakedness
              in a field
of light

BLACK PIETY

The Blackfriars
murmur prayers, kneeling
in a circle

They have not seen
the silver legs
dancing in the sunlight

They have not seen
the golden feet
rhythmical and perfect

Will God sustain
the slander
their blind piety flaunts?

Your broad

Band of
          deep red
holding

Your roiled
          dark
hair away

From your
          silver
spurred

Ears
     the number
of bones

In your
          bared back
interests me

As well
          as your
green eyes

You're sparing
              a chance
or two

This is

The place
it is a
rock place

You hug your
knees shivering

Your long tresses
cover modicum
flesh, the stones
cover the stones

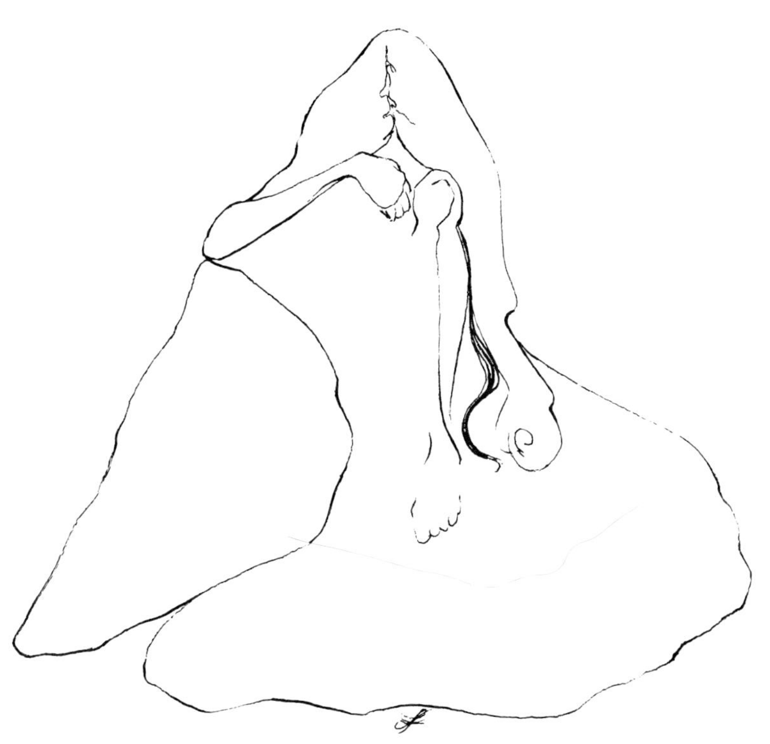

Your eyes

Seem very
gentle, though
there seems
a third between
the other two

I'm not used
to girls
that kind

The startled

Montage
            your
belly now

Seems
        salted
marrow

Waiting
        shadowed
sure

To shed
        its
mask

Where

The flesh
          of your face
gives way
          to the flesh
of your lips

Is a delicate zone
                    of strange
mutations
          and wonderous
rewards

Where
        the hairy flesh
of your mons
                  gives way
to the moist meat
                    of
the lips
        of your vulva

shocks
        every nerve
of tongue
        and eye and
finger tip
        of the
heart's
        very
core

As
   sudden rain forests
giving way
        to sudden
grottos
        and to
sea

Sleep

Swollen
you rear
awake

Reaching
with
liquid arms

A liquid
tongue
voice

Incapacitated
but for
receiving

Stone over

Stone
        and the far hills that are
mountains rising up
                        through a nimbus
of white mist struck by sunlight

These large stones
                        shaped by water
and frost-etched. Some split
as by a mighty blow, some jagged

But sustained by soil
                        some vegetation
and the hills there, to reach out to
the mist sucked away
toward deep canyons

I read

Your erotic poem
and then
            found myself
absentmindedly
lipping the binding
of your book

The taste of that
putrid glue
            only half
bringing me
back
to my senses

In the rubble

Where all lost jewels are reposited
                              the skin
of a snake, a rat's skull, a turd
sprouting a bean-stalk that might grow up
to no telling where
                    where my memory of you is
daunted by my memory of doubt
                                    doubting
your thighs opulent of mercy
doubting the thin treble of your
thin voice
          noosing me mightily
                        your thighs
were not thin
they would have noosed me forever
I trashed it
          but
the memory is still there

Objects

Of weather
            the weather of the mind
her brow intent, looking to the sea
she has looked for many years
the wind sways her black shawl

It was first a husband
                    then a son
now she looks to the sea
for the sea is hers
for none can take it away

It has not

Departed
simply
for having shut
your eyes

It will not
depart
because the sun
is down
or the lights
are out

Do you think it
will depart

Because
you're dead

The freak

Of late light
on rocks and sand—
my freaked eye seeking
a moral metaphor
to do it no good

Your torso
is a freak of light
rising and walking
my moral metaphors
are great
                and
dim

Visions

Of water and where it is ended
of gardens and the last of flowers

The sea is like glass molten
the great sun bronze there

On its centre naked as the belly
of a dancer but the garden

Is denuded the flower gatherers
are making wreaths for the day

To give glory to the dead
I would give glory to the sun the sea

Conrad, I shouted

As my
        comrade
fell but I

Knew he
        had out
lasted

His vigour
        and on
they came

Shouting
        black
nigger

Black
    nigger I
lifted a

White flag
        at last
trusting I'd

Be treated
        like a
lady

Pungent, boiling

Tar
    a stench of childhood
road repair
so cotton wagons could move
two abreast
            though never did
or trucks could pass, going slow
if you swore by magic

We gathered truant blobs
or strings of it to burn
in small ovens jugged
in the embankment

The smoke was black and ominous
the boiling, bubbling, and burning
satanic
        there in the South
it still had other
more satanic
uses
in that day

This wheel

Or hoop
       a bicycle
rim with

No spokes
       on the
American

Desert out
       beyond
Gallup

It's likely
       to last
till

The red
       man
returns

Chances are
       a long
time

THE KEY

First I
        put it in
my mouth

Then
        up my
ass

The detectives
                were
on their way

First they
        raised the
window shade

Then
        lowered it
again

Ran a finger
          through
the dust

On the polished
               mahogany
end table

Of course
          the lock
was broken

But I had
          burned all
the papers

I am

Accused of
            having
eyes, of

Turning
        my
head

Around—
            there
are

Remedies
        for such
offences

I applied

My own
      remedy
of wart

Medicine
      behind
my ear

For
  seven
days

But certain
      family
members

Hinted
   a lob-
otomy

Would do
     the job
as well

The vision of

Every naked, wrenched limb
bark-stripped
                the trunk as well
and each convoluted twig
a giant tree
                dead
still standing
its strength and dignity
never
gone out of it

Its beauty
against the sky
more awesome than the remains
of sentient man
                or his
kindred creatures beaten down
by pain
before they die

Finally

I
 decided
I'd

Eat
    what I
like

No
     mat-
ter

How
      it
smells

The ocean

Of moon
            I'll transfigure
the habitat of mourning

I'll bring down
the dragon out of the rafters

I'll graft lions' beards
to monkeys' chins

I'll teach the parrot
pidgin Chinese

My next bride will have
cunt lips
like a cobra's hood

My mode

Of travel
            I put
a thimble on my
finger

And dial
a distant
number

It all comes back
glick tongue
somewhere
next December

The tip

Of your
          penis
is a

Small rosebud
               pink
& self-contained

It grows
          visibly beneath
my sight

One petal
          rolls
back

It is pinker
          and larger
but it

Is still
     a rosebud
self-contained

Wind

That can neither sweep
me away
nor let me rest

That kind of
nagging love is
the kind of love

I've gotten
by with

Getting by
barely getting by

I have not

Climbed
        that high up
where the bells cluster
and their din
is a thick void you
could not cut with spite

If I did
        I'd no doubt be
clapping my wings
like all tired virgins
and looking for
a nest for the night

I knew

Empirically
          that
her legs

Weren't
          just words
but I

Began
        to wonder if
her cunt

Was not
          just
a vague

Gloss
      she had
read

Over
      quickly
in a

Medical
          book never
believed

The succinct

Web I broke through
your mind
          to confront—
a crucifix dangling
my cock
nailed to it

I fucked

Her
   twice
found out she
was a Christer
wanted to save
my soul
next Sunday

Suspended

Naked on
            your handsome haunches
as if prepared to begin
a Russian dance
                    your jaunty thighs
expose a comfortable snatch
                            by any ample
calculation, firm buttocks
a deep navel

What good breasts and round arms
the spine erect, the neck somewhat
skewed to lend a hauteur
                        that is charming
a hauteur the body
                itself
does not suggest

Your tapestry

Of a cat
            her smiling face
like your own
                her rich pelt
all engulfing
as your own brocade

If your honest hand
would strip your face away
if an honest God
should strip you bare

Touching you

With my mouth
without eyes or hands

What geography
of your being
could I construct

More than even
a burning bush

I would be
startled
to learn that it
could speak

Your de-

Ceptive
        symmetry
you'd

Have
      me be-
lieve

You've
        a heart
be-

Neath
        each
boob

Where

Was I
        that day
last week you did
up your hair
different from before

You may never
have known
I noticed
            but I
looked in
the window
went past

Figured you
had found
a new beau

The obedience

Of my umbrella
in a high wind
is less contrived
than this blarney
you feed me on
day and night

I'll never take you
out in a high wind
I'd never untangle
what was you
from the bedding
or the bedsprings
or your ass

I didn't set

Out to
        break
your heart

Only
     if I
could

Break
        a few
bones

The night is

Over
        and nothing
was accomplished
though the dream-work
wracked my psyche
and my bones
ache as well

The sheets are spotted
with sperm
though no image
was an image
of beauty
and none erotic

The day's work will be
almost as arduous
and its final end as banal

I wouldn't think

Of writing
            a poem
when

My wife
            is in
the house

Any more
            than I
would think

Of bringing
            another woman
to the house

When she
            is not
there

I think
        of it
but

I soon
        dismiss
the notion

I won't try

To shield her from the mess
I've made
            if I cleaned it
up too quickly
she would never believe it
ever happened

Two tiers

Of door-
          ways a
collapsible

Frame—
          your mirror
image

Is a
     Mayan
coin—

I spent
          doubloons
to burn

The
     house
down

Maybe it is

My funeral
            but
at least

There's
        a good deal
of noise

And maybe
            you'll notice
the corpse

Isn't doing
            much of
the weeping

I get

Drunk
        and write
poetry

Like
    I thought
it

Was
    cardinal
sin

STAID

My memory which she left
in tatters
          there you have
the melodrama of it

Say I walked with her
in the damp twilight
                    plum blossoms
suffusing the air

She was talking
                her voice husky
vibrant
in her slender throat

She was speaking of Einstein
and relativity

Perchance
          her truth
possesses as much validity
as my own

If your cunt   56

Did not exist
                I would
invent it

So it is
        right now
as you

Well know
            three-fifths
or so pure

Invention
            I'll not apply
for a patent

I'd like
        the thought
to get

Into
    the public
domain

Some substance

Of possibility
            straining the certitudes
of your white form
                    as you chose
to put
your clothes back on

I have chosen to put down also
                            my pen
my paints, my fucking certitude

We start out afresh, arms bared
                            waiting
for suppertime
                waiting
for the telephone to ring

These possibilities
                    straining for substance
straining for a certitude

If I had

Worn out
          the tip end of
my middle finger
fooling with the cunts of
a few dear friends

I would say
          okay
it's worn out

The fact of the matter is
it has
a hell of a lot more wear
left in it

Red-mouthed

Boys
        hugging
early dawn's chill
about their thin chests

They've got
the Early Morning
Edition and
they know it will sell

Titles by Wings Press:

Bonazzi, Robert **Fictive Music**
Bright, Susan **julia**
Crews, Judson **Nolo Contendere**
Crockett, Eleanor Earle **Two Poems**
Fowler, David Gene **Brief Case**
McGee, M.W. **Ambrosia Dancing at Mary's**
Miller, Vassar **Approaching Nada**
Miller, Vassar **Small Change**
Plumb, David **The Music Stopped and Your Monkey's On Fire**
Van Zandt, Townes **For the Sake of the Song**
Ventura, Michael **The Mollyhawk Poems**
Winans, A.D. **Venus in Pisces**